These Are the People in Your Neighbourhood

Fredericton poems

by
Jordan Trethewey
City of Fredericton Poet Laureate (2021-2024)

ROADSIDE PRESS

Roadside Press
Meredosia, Illinois

Contents

Eva Christensen
Learning to Walk, Again
2023

Watercolour on paper
12 x 16 inches

Foreword I

The meaning we search for
all our lives, is happening.
Now. We just don't notice it.

There is significance in stories
from all lives in progress.
These poems make obvious
the incognito utterances beneath
our day-to-day existence.

I need community—big, or small.
I want to connect.
I need someone to remember.

Foreword II: Good Friday at The Cap

Everyone has a nondenominational story.
At least, I hope so.

What is life, but a collection—
stories imperfectly bound

together? This project could be
a reflection of community.

No bag of words, no costume trunk.
*Full of freaks and disenfranchised punks**

who aren't here in the light
of religious holiday, it seems

they only come out at night,
hoot 'n' holler, stomp the boards

when it's time to drink oblivion,
vent pressurized life-gasses

to local and national melodies,
while crafty nano brew snakes

its way through liquid lines
as brewers dodge dodgy keg

spikes. I wait in anticipation,
of words, meaningful and new,

to beat into this old laptop,
words that could bring

those who read them together
in greater understanding of

the people, and place, they've chosen
to live in all these years,

but are too busy to meet
and explore. It's possible to open

sun-bleached curtains to permit
collaboration and understanding

to germinate. Looking out at Queen
Street on a Good Friday, one can hope.

*lyrics from "An Inch an Hour," by The Tragically Hip

Essential Writing
for Carlos Morales

If you were a writer
with a social conscience
in El Salvador during the civil war,
you wrote what you saw—
the injustice all around.

Carlos worked part-time
in San Salvador's National Art Gallery
while studying Spanish literature.
A time of great personal growth
soon cut short.

A fledgling poet, he admits
to inauspicious beginnings,
imitating his friend's style,
while finding his own voice
in a writers group—Patriaexacta.

Carlos meets a musician friend
one afternoon at a café
in his home town to discuss
pairing his poems with music.
Meanwhile, police and military lurk

nearby, waiting to arrest someone,
anyone for trumped-up treason.
He doesn't know what gave them away
as possible conspirators—where they sat,
what they said, or how they walked.

Suddenly, they were surrounded.
Swarmed by armed officers.
Making matters worse,
Carlos' smoking gun, his poems,

rested inside his bag
radiating dissent.
To commit opinions to paper
in 1980s El Salvador,
meant NEVER attaching
a God-given name to it.

Life's work confiscated,
Carlos spent two immobile weeks
blindfolded in a tiny cell
with 30 other political prisoners.
Monotony broken only by

bouts of interrogation enacted
by a shadow government
afraid of eventual retribution.
In Santa Tecla, an anxious mother
begs influential acquaintances

to intervene—a letter
to the president's wife
from her former teacher
vouches for Carlos' character.
Interrogations stop.

Week Three—Carlos regains sight,
set loose among the gen. pop.
He spends hours reading. Writes for inmates.
Hides new poems in his underwear
until released, days later.

Eyes wide open, Carlos knows
he can't un-see, un-know.
Must bear witness to oppressive
homeland realities. Must connect
memory and image with paper,

despite persistent persecution of family.
Even when emigration becomes necessity.
In the end, a beginning—new nation,
new language. A place that welcomes
the truth of words.

Reflecting Light into Dark Places
for Outreach Staff and clients of Liberty Lane

I

There are so many decisions to make
in the dark, sometimes you freeze—
unable to connect one neuron to the next,
put right foot ahead of the left,

move along at even a snail's pace.
We know it intuitively as kids—
horrible things fester and creep
in the absence of light at night.

As we grow, convinced by trusted adults
of our foolishness, we are embarrassed;
persuaded to squash the natural urge
for fight or flight— ignore intuition.

A blanket absence of safety descends
without resistance. Without light,
negative corners surround, entrap hope
with the swelling embrace of fists,

words that slice away self-esteem.
Mole-like eyes become accustomed
to living in the dark. When the first
dust motes dance through curtain cracks,

we wonder whether to hide—
if it's just another beautiful lie.
You marvel at the possibility,
some strangers are willing

to waltz right in—care, listen,
validate as required. It's true,

Black Holes do devour light, but
not everything is a mathematical equation.

Darkness tucks tail—
disappears like cowardly vampires
in the presence of unguarded individuals
armed only with daylight and mirror.

II

We see you—your circumstance,
trauma camped within your body,
the bravery to seek a distant bunker
outside the war zone.

One day you woke up inside a pit,
didn't know how you got there.
We see you—waving,
but cannot pull you out.

Triage by a few in service of many
locked, isolated in a sick society's
bear hug embrace. The wicked
never rest, so no rest for us

mitigating rot in floorboards—
a silent pandemic beneath headline crisis.
We forge on without front-line funding.
Witness resilient responses to loaded questions

peppered with preconceived viewpoints
designed to keep you in place—
"No. I've told you five times,
that is not what happened."

We are "Little C" counsellors
with "Big C" compassion, walking

beside you without judgement,
carrying scissors to cut red tape.

We realize the expert on your life is you.
Need a rope? We have a sturdy one,
carefully knotted at manageable intervals,
supporting the decision to climb.

Something Different About Me
for Randall Haslett

Randall's grandmother tells him,
There's something different about you,
yet he appears no different than his siblings.

For 16 years, he wonders what it might be.
Mother's gift that year, an origin story.
She explains, the Canadian military man

you call Dad, is actually Step-Dad.
Biologically, Randall's a dual citizen,
the son of an American purser who died

aboard Northwest Airlines Flight 4422
when it crashed into 16,000-foot Mt. Sanford
in 1948, ferrying off-duty merchant mariners

from Singapore to New Jersey for OTS Oil.
His mother was to meet
her husband of three years in Chicago.

He never left Alaska. Eager to get home,
pilot took an unauthorized shortcut at 11,000 feet.
Flew into Alaska's sixth-highest peak.

A 13-year-old girl, working in Anchorage
at a movie theatre canteen, confirmed
the explosive outcome for all aboard.

II

Randall never thought the glacier
would reveal Flight 4422's secrets.
Enter Global Warming, and two pilots

whose hobby is aircraft investigation
cold cases. On a 1998 hike up Mt. Sanford,
during the July-August safe window,

they find a frozen arm
resting at 8,000 feet,
believe it belongs to Randall's father.

The search for living next of kin begins.
In 2011, Randall is invited
to explore the debris field.

An adventure-trained, Canadian
Artillery veteran, Randall relaxes
in his element.

The glacier relinquishes
Flight 4422's propeller. He holds it,
one of the last things his father saw.

Eva Christensen
Every Silver Lining Has a Touch of Grey
2023

Gouache on paper
18 x 18 inches

Use pliers and a wood screw
for Diane Reid

Ian advises, if you find
yourself in a wine emergency—
no corkscrew.

Linda returns to her 4th Floor
apartment, with this odd,
yet useful, information.

Her roommate, Diane, paces,
waits to hear if her ruse
was successful in uncovering

the availability of four
young men who just moved
into the apartment below.

***

We need to meet them, Diane says,
after meeting one handsome lad
on her way up in the elevator.

- How?
- Ask to borrow a corkscrew.
- But we have one.

Linda is a busty young blonde.
Diane knows she'll be irresistible
in her white pyjama dress with

flowing rainbow ribbon. But only one-fourth
of the new mailbox nameplate is home.
And no corkscrew.
But Ian is a trouble shooter,

offers Linda an alternative
method for a desperate situation.

***

Diane grew up in Vancouver,
shares an apartment with Linda
inside the same brick building where,
outside, she used to gather horse
chestnuts to huck at her little brother.

Earlier in the year, pregnant
and single, she chooses
to keep her baby. *Why not?*
She has a well-paid job,
works night shifts

helping West Coast customers
make travel plans with Air Canada.
Linda's birth story—the opposite.
Her baby, adopted out. She works
days, babysits Diane's son at night.

***

A few nights post corkscrew scam,
the ladies receive an invite
to party with the boys below.

Not knowing who is who, Diane
is struck by a tall, handsome man
wearing a UBC football cap—

Coach Ian, talking
to another beautiful woman. Still,
she cannot take her eyes off him,

despite a tenacious pursuit
by Cute Elevator Guy, who
no longer captures her fancy.

Throughout the following year,
Ian and Diane are inseparable.
He evolves effortlessly into father figure.

Is there for baby's first steps.
Is there when she cuts her finger
slicing roast beef.

Hears her joke about being lucky
she didn't sever her ring finger
completely, still hoping

to wear a gold band
with diamond solitaire
one day. Ian reaches

in his ubiquitous gym bag,
crouches on one knee,
You mean, like this?

***

On their wedding day,
Linda approaches the couple
with her gift

in a velvet ring box.
Diane opens it, reveals
the serendipitous screw,

with a note
that reads—
Best screw I ever had!

Mrs. Mills Marvels
For Lucinda Mills

Mrs. Mills teaches middle school Art.
Mohammed doesn't speak English,
yet becomes talkative (through Arabic
friend's translation) when he sees
her classroom sewing machine.

Not part of her curriculum, yet
she's inspired to let him show
what he knows. Fabric provided,
the 13-year-old admits to making
pants for 5 years. Will try his best

to make the sweater for his friend.
A thank-you. Mrs. Mills marvels
at Mohammed's skill, acquired
via questionable circumstances,
or necessity. And it is perfect.

I Repeat, Crystal is Down!
for Tina Trethewey

There's no business like show business.
Ask former amusement park mascot, Tina.
You might not recognize her from her role
as Crystal Palace's Crystal, circa 1998.

A summer job at an amusement park,
every student's dream. After graduating
mascot school, Tina is paired with a Buddy
to help with sight line issues caused

by an oversized foam head. Suited-up
for her first non-speaking performance,
Tina exits the glamorous storage closet.
Only able to look straight ahead,

she doesn't notice her Buddy is high,
deep in contemplation of closet wall.
As the door clicks shut, she steps
into an off-limits area of the park,

under the rattling roller coaster.
There, she is greeted by three, overly-
enthusiastic teen boys, *Hi, Crystal!*
We are so excited to see you!

Tina turns her actual head, sees
only the inside of the costume, feels
the costume's red yarn pigtails being
whipped in an attempt to dislodge

the head. The hooligans soon realize
it won't come off. They start to shove
the oversized noggin back-and-forth
until Tina falls over. Her cries for help

drowned by the coaster's clank.
Her skull and body saved
from the beating that follows
by the padded costume.

The kicks to her legs cost her two day's
work. Eventually, stoner Buddy
arrives, *Hey, what's going on, guys?*
Mascot assassins flee the scene

as the hero yells into his walkie talkie,
Crystal is down! I repeat, Crystal...is...down!
The unfamiliar code alerts the manager,
who helps Tina out of the straightjacket.

Stoner Buddy pursues assailants
in the wrong direction, is reassigned
to the arcade as game token distributor.
Where wandering is an asset.

The Big Red Chair
for April Robinson

Nine-year-old girls fall in love with
the strangest things. An antique
red velvet chair, for instance,
first foisted on parents by an uncle
who earned it in exchange
for a day's yard work labour.

Mother is prepared for many things
to make grand re-entries in her life.
She never expects the Big Red Chair
to be one of them, as she places it
in her annual yard sale.

April sits on the chair the whole day,
hopes to prevent an upsetting sale.
A Cambridge-Narrows man sees
past the determined squatter, notes
what she did: something beautiful.

Two deals are brokered that day,
payment for the Big Red Chair,
and a promise to April, it will be hers
when he is no longer enamoured.

Ten years pass. April finishes year two
at Mount Alison. The phone rings.
The Big Red Chair not only re-enters
April's life, but her mother's as well,
like the proverbial cat, bad penny, and ex-boyfriend.
Her little girl, a nomadic student after all.

Post university, and a trip to Ireland,
April barely settles in Ottawa
before her mother visits
bearing the Big Red Chair.

Like a steadfast sister,
the Big Red Chair remains
by April's side, follows her
through the good and bad,
a stop in Quebec, and a divorce,
before closing the circle back
in Fredericton no worse for wear.
Sporting new upholstery
to compliment new perspective.

Don't Call Me Stupid
for Amie Kitts

How we handle ourselves
in a seemingly small crisis
can have a huge impact
on the person in turmoil.

At 11, Amie wants to like sports,
but spatial and hand-eye hindrances
cause collapse on playing fields.
Wrong place, wrong time, every time.

She wants to compete
rain or shine, but melts down
when wet (showers exempt).
Neuro-divergent blue butterfly effect.

Waning days of fifth grade bring
traditional Track & Field day.
Always overcast and angsty,
mist and rain on and off again.

As dry duds absorb water weight,
darkness clouds Amie's thoughts
until the squishy squash of soggy shoes
becomes maniacal metronome.

Unable to cope in a situation
she can't leave, three years' acquired
calm forgotten: *I'll blow up that school
if you don't get me out of the rain!*

Response to idle threat
from frustrated teacher,
Shut-up! That's stupid talk!
Drags pre-teen sobbing,

screaming to next event.
Her reserve of remaining confidence
in intellect, is crushed. Amie weeps,
I just want go home.

Desperate wishes are sometimes granted
to those in desperate need.
Her mother swoops in with the cure:
dry clothes, and food.

Takes her to work, a studio
where broadcaster mom records
audio for a political campaign.
Amie tries it, too. Has fun.

Her mother's daytime confidence,
an inspiring antidote to earlier
dismantling of her ego—Amie's
dramatic introduction to daily contradiction.

Shit can hit the fan before sunshine,
malevolence can mask misunderstanding,
regret can lead to reconciliation, and
being called stupid, doesn't mean you are.

Eva Christensen
All Day Breakfast
2021

Watercolour on paper
16 x 20 inches
Private Collection

Not Something She Usually Does
for Mary McKenna

The young man looks forlorn
underneath the Westmorland
Street off-ramp. Mary stops
asks if he needs anything.
Not something she usually does.

The young man asks for a hug.
Mary avoids the subject,
continues to chat.
Conversation returns to the hug.
She sees the dead end in his eyes,

steps in for an embrace—
not something she usually does.
Asks if he needs anything else.
He steps back. Smiles.
No. Thank you.

If a tree snaps
for Raven Simon

in the woods at night
and only one stoned person
is there to hear it,
might there be two people?

Raven is homeless,
heavily into drugs.
One night, he runs
into the forest.

When he hears
the unmistakeable CRACK
of splintering wood,
he feels watched.

Without words,
no another sound,
something speaks to Raven.
A ghostly presence tangoes

with his subconscious
until an epiphany comes
bubbling to the surface
of his freshly sober mind—

CLEAN UP.
So he does.
Where once was a void,
now stands a man

with thoughts about Creation,
belief in equilibrium,
a spiritual understanding,
he does exist.

Visibility on Temperance Street
for Brian Nelligan

Brian and Transportation agree to disagree
on evidence that planes, trains, and automobiles
all tried to kill him at one time, or another.
Dates of incredible trauma imprint themselves

on our minds. May 6, 1987, 18-year-old
air cadet flight sergeant Brian, and five
friends, leave drill training in Westville, N.S.
at 9 pm. They take a different route home.

Brian and pal Darrell chat in the back,
while Alta takes unlit Temperance Street,
trees hugging the road. As they approach
the train crossing known locally as

Dukes of Hazzard Tracks, they wonder,
for just a moment, why a car is parked
in the opposite lane, facing them
beyond the crossing.

Headlights on trains have a blind spot
of 150 metres. They never saw it.
Too close. It didn't blow its whistle
on approach. They never heard it

until the moment Brian saw
the behemoth at Darrell's right-
rear passenger window.
Now he is terrified of train whistles.

Accident scene measurements include:
total airborne distance traveled, 200 feet;
peak height while airborne (according to
witness in parked car) 50 feet.

The car lands on its wheels,
Brian's head goes through left-rear
passenger window. Bloody, and
in shock, his flight response kicks in.

He shoves his way out of the vehicle.
Runs, thinking the car will explode
from sparks created by the train.
His friends cry for him to return, help them.

Fuck you guys, I'm living through this!
Brian sees the bystander run to the car.
It's still running, but not on fire. He races back,
turns it off, helps his friends out, and away.

Sirens approach to assess concussions.
A volunteer fireman tells Brian he's bleeding.
Brian passes out from the sight.
Accusations of stunt racing, partying

begin immediately, but witness corroborates
teens' story. No warning whistle. The six lucky
passengers remain close. Trees cut back.
Visibility on Temperance Street improves.

Happiness is a Place
for Heather Desjardins

Molly is 13-and-a-half years old.
In that time, she's had:
a knee replaced,
developed cataracts,
gone stone deaf.

On summer vacations at the camp,
she returns to the days of youth.
When family sedan tires hit
familiar dirt road, she feels
rejuvenated, knows she's there.

With a little help, she hops
down lakeshore stairs,
relaxes, the damage of gravity
briefly suspended,
a happy puppy again at 91.

Head West, Young Girls
for Auralia Brooke

Would you rather:
A) Travel around the world once
then return home, or
B) Move to the West Coast
permanently?

Auralia and her mother are a pair.
Although she's just 4 years old,
her mother trusts her judgement.
When daughter chooses Pacific Ocean,
mother begins packing their bags
to leave Ontario forever.

Mother's savings only last so long.
At a Vancouver hostel, if not sleeping,
or washing dishes to pay for their stay,
they walk the city during a transit strike.
Auralia reads her first word: VACANCY,
while looking for a new home.

Suffers her first indignation when lumped
into the same red-light rental category as pets.
Auralia believes in her mother implicitly,
they reached the coast as promised.
If her mother's not worried,
she suspects smooth sailing ahead.

Eva Christensen
July Afternoon at Carleton and Queen
2023

Watercolour on paper
10 x 10 inches
Private Collection

Not a Soft Person
for Dai Pham

It cost Dai Pham a lot
to travel to New Brunswick
from Vietnam. The oldest son
of poor parents, he sifted airfare
and tuition through sheer grit.

Logistics of long distance
relationships are like algebra
for lovers, even harder
for grown children and parents.

How can they see
your successes, the fruits
of academic and practical pursuits?
How can you look after them
when you are 180 degrees apart?

Comfort cannot bounce off satellites,
travel under oceans, when you relate
how you rose above the moment
at Home Depot, attempting to help
a confused customer who says,
Don't touch me! Go back
to the country you came from!

It twists your guts,
makes you wail and weep
into pillows, disconnecting
a long-distance call
to a mother who cannot
answer the question,
Do you know who I am?
Or, when you relive

the moment of your first-
hand experience with racism
in the country you chose
to blaze your own trail in
without familial safety net.

Dad did time at 21.
Never told his son
about the crime.
Dai envisions the prison
tattoos that cover angry muscles
when he phones. A father's
advice: *be a good person.*
Not like me.

A question nags at Dai's core:
who am I, if family forgets me?
Silent sobs communicate
love that transcends personal
history, accepts remorse.

Once She Loves
for Yess Enm

We all live life assuming that others
live exactly as we do. Yess can't lie,
can't live with anxiety. Can't hide what
is written on her face. She's been single,

and single with kids. Been dumped, more
than she's left. Spent five years loving a cold man.
Kids wanted a Dad. And he never lied—if
married, it's an agreement, not passion.

Is her heart big enough for a third, a man-child?
Decides—not quite. Three single years tick by.
Meets a new ego needing validation post-breakup.
Yess assumes trust, discovers trysts.

Her heart's too big to close. Once she loves you,
she cannot turn it off. Will never stop.

Torn from Food Magazines
for Stephanie Sedgewick

Stephanie hears a wet smooching sound
followed by stifled giggles. She looks up.
The roughest boy in the room holds the torn

image of a woman's thonged buttocks
in one hand, a torn pair of lips in the other,
as he pantomimes a nine year old's idea

of consenting adults having a good time.
Mortified that rumours might spread
about the new teacher, Stephanie

halts collage time. Confiscates the boy's
magazine, now redacted of all female
anatomy, clothed, or otherwise.

***

Teaching in a foreign environment,
devoid of necessities, like books,
a good teacher will improvise.

Stephanie can't find teaching work
in Fredericton. Again. She packs up.
Again. Returns to small coastal village

in Nunavut. To Grade 4/5 split.
Outbound teacher leaves stack of food
magazines for use in the bare classroom.

Stephanie distributes for Healthy Choices
collage. Didn't flip through. Returns to
her desk. Fifteen minutes pass when...

Helping People Find Shit
for Julia Stewart

Julia's done it her whole working life—
first as an Eastern Canadian tour guide,
now as director of Fredericton Public Library.

If you ask her parents
which of their children
might become a librarian,

neither would say Julia.
Why does a gregarious tour guide
switch gears, become a library boss?

Doctor's orders. M.S. patients
cannot manage chronic illness
while traveling six months of the year.

Which sucks. Julia is an expert
at standing backwards on busses,
speaks expertly about places

she can't see coming—a dream
job for an extrovert who would have
continued it happily into her dotage.

***

Instead, she takes her savings
from one career, parlays it
into a Master's of Library Science.

Libraries are not natural
stomping grounds for the bombastic,
but Julia is not interested

in working corridors of condescension,
cloistered in academic alcoves.
Talk of buildings that house books

still feels strange to someone who
never cocooned herself in stacks.
Back when schools were constructed

with books in mind, Julia had good fortune
to find Mrs. Sims reading kids stories at lunch,
suggesting books. Her family,

from grandparents on down—all readers.
Little wonder she cannot sleep
without a book in her hands.

***

Julia is the only student in her class
to do her practicum in a public library.
A perfect place for a people person

who loves to read, and easily finds shit.
Her first boss puts it bluntly at her interview,
I can teach anyone about library stuff,

but not how to talk to people.
It was a match. The library in Sackville,
N.S., soon experiences a demographic shift

as Halifax leans into gentrification,
the poor forced into the suburbs,
the little library becomes

de-facto drop-in centre, a place
where at-risk youth feel safe.
This comes with a variety of baggage

librarians are not trained to deal with.
Librarians not named Julia, that is.
Naturally personable and inquisitive,

she listens, has just one rule:
respect—for yourself, and others.
Key concept when you find

a 10-year-old sleeping under a desk.
Don't yell, or accuse.
Ask, *What's wrong?*

Hand them a snack.
This child sleeps here
for reasons too dark to articulate.

Julia's transformation now complete—
outspoken fact-slinger, into empathetic listener.
Necessary for managing any public service.

Which Dad is Which?
for Corenski Nowlan

There is a game
Corenski plays
with his partner.

It begins

each time he hangs
up with his step-dad
or biological father.

I just got off the phone
with my dad.

Which one?

The alcoholic.

Which one?

The one dying.

Which one?

The one who needs an organ transplant.

Which one?

The one who mistreated my mother.

Which one?

The one who abandoned me.

Oh. THAT one.

Eva Christensen
Freddy Beach
2023

Watercolour on paper
8 x 10 inches

Daughter, please...
for Izzy Trethewey

always make those sounds
that make me laugh

contort your face in ways
I find hard to mimic

enjoy your food
with curiosity and abandon

continue to take on every experience
without worry of falling on your butt

keep your unrestrained, belly-first canter
when initiating new friendships

allow yourself to laugh
and cry at the same time

scream to get my attention
if I remain oblivious to your needs

don't stop talking—
I'll listen, even if I don't understand

Dad's intuition only grows from
witness to what his daughter says and does

so, please,
don't hide yourself away

Potential Indian Husband
for Likhita Potluri

When an Indian girl turns 19,
her mother's thoughts turn
to arranged marriage.

She pulls out her address book,
begins calling relatives
with sons of marrying age.

In no time, Likhita's mother
finds an eligible cousin
who appraises the merchandise,

offers cash to mother,
an iPhone to daughter,
to seal the deal.

Likhita immediately vetoes.
But potential Indian husbands
are not easily rebuffed.

The pursuant buyer persists.
Likhita enlists a male friend
to pretend he's a cop

investigating harassment complaint.
The cousin ceases and desists,
but not before informing their family

of her charges against him,
now rumoured to be the cause
of the uncle's heart attack.

Last Fatal Duel in New Brunswick
for the Village of New Maryland

In 1821, a mistaken identity, slip of the tongue
led to arrest of Smith Senior, not Junior, the son.

Barrister Street made an unfortunate slip,
then admitted to his error, double-quick.

He ordered a jury compensate the accused.
Procedural tape left two lawyers unamused.

Outside the York courthouse there rose a great fuss.
George Wetmore, Senior's lawyer, threatened and cussed.

Feeling his honor irreparably damaged,
Wetmore sent Street a formal duel challenge.

In a clearing atop Maryland Hill, October the second,
Wetmore would have his besmirched dignity reckoned.

Witnesses loaded the pistols, measured the paces.
The main combatants then took their places.

Weapons at sides until ordered to fire.
Both raised their arms quickly at target desired.

First shots broke cold silence, both men stood unhurt.
After their second, George Wetmore's blood did spurt.

Wetmore gasped his last breath. Street rode for the border.
Months later returning to answer for murder.

All parties agreed to cover this shame.
Both Wetmore and Street were equal in blame.

Street later wrote—honour is dearer than life.
Yet he went to his grave never telling his wife.

Mother's Fault
for Ebba Hamer

To a Grade 11 German exchange student
from Hanover, Fredericton gives off
a vibe both exciting and scary.

Like every teenager, Ebba blames
her mother for most things,
especially the desire

to visit an English-speaking country.
Mom's 3 months in Winnipeg
turned into a lifelong friendship

with her exchange partner.
Tales from this time fill Ebba's head
with the real possibility of having

her own exotic adventures.
In the post-pandemic fall of 2022,
things are different for Ebba.

The world feels closed to kindness.
Strange ridicule for those like her
who play it safe, wear medical masks.

Hailed as life savers mere months ago.
Without an exchange partner visiting
Germany, there is no one to trade

fish out of water tales with,
to stifle her homesickness with a laugh.
So, Ebba spoils her host family

with German baking when not buried
in books, or thinking about Christmas
without loved ones near.

Eva Christensen
This Perspective Isn't Fixed
2022

Watercolour and gouache on paper
16 x 20 inches

A King's Breakfast
for Craig Moir

Craig is always busy
ignoring his alarm clock
at 6:30 in the morning.

This particular morning,
still in the thrall of Snooze,
he hears an strange yowl

emanating from the living room.
He reluctantly rubs his eyes,
discovers his elderly cat, Hera,

proudly proclaiming a fresh kill.
Seeing her master, Hera
tosses it at his feet,

proof of her fealty
and perennial youth.
Hera, mighty lioness,

devours her breakfast
with snaps, crackles, and pops
that make the king of the castle

forget his Rice Krispies.
Mistaking his fascination
for desire to partake,

Hera bestows upon King Craig
an offering of gizzard.
The best part.

This is the Path
for Cassandra LeBlanc

Who is Cassandra,
now that the constructs,
religion and marriage,
are forsaken?

Turns out, enjoyable conversation
is just an on ramp to
Lifelong Relationship Road.
Not the whole highway.

***

Cassandra wants to belong within
a church's comforting embrace,
but isn't offered a chance
to play piano inside God's house.

When her best friend proposes
celibate courtship, at 18,
leading to good Christian matrimony,
she thinks, *Why not? This is the path.*

***

You know, I never really believed in God,
she blurts, on a Penniac back road,
driver and engine thrown in reverse.
If you don't believe in the man upstairs,

what do you believe?
An important question
husband and wife discuss
without animosity, or shame.

***

Her husband also realizes he never bought
a ticket to paradise in the clouds either.
Once a foundation cracks,
the house shifts, separates, divides.

There is an Animal in My Brain
for Misha Milchenko

What if I'm the first
to die, jumping off
the 25-foot rock ledge,
at this abandoned quarry
filled with goldfish
called The Cuts?

Misha takes a cursory walk
around the sheer face
of the circular pit rippling
orange on the surface,
contemplates mortality.

A mistake. Fear enjoys
circumventing philosophy.
The first jump was a breeze,
no scarier than a diving board.

Further up, the 25-foot
medium drop. Courage high,
Misha convinces himself
he is Braveheart
after five baby dives.

All day, dozens take
this plunge without injury.
Not quite ready,
he walks further. Higher
to the 40-foot launch pad
local legend and graffiti,
confirm is a real killer.

Proud of his rational mind,
Misha realizes high school kids

have survived the medium jump
all day, but he's never
faced his fear of heights.

The wind feels
stronger at this height.
Doesn't it?

People jump, over
and over, laughing,
but there's an animal
in his brain, saying,
You're gonna die!

Thirty minutes pass.
Misha sees a girl
having second-thoughts
as well. He thinks,
if she does it,
I will. She doesn't.

After an hour,
an acquaintance decides
to assist by jumping, too.
But she freezes.

Misha formulates another plan,
asks this woman to count
down from 10. The simple math
clears his mind, narrows his focus.

Zero!
He jumps, finishes
in a perfect Ass-Cracker.
He swims back to shore,
risk its own reward.
Nothing left to prove.
Time for potato chips.

Do Not Dismiss
for Grace Bowness

There is a limit to everything.
Especially disrespect.
Grace has drive. Work ethic
daily proof of capability.
She pursued a degree,
Chemical Engineering,
to silence dismissive doubters
in a male-dominated field.

No matter how much drive you possess,
even high-performance engines can crack
when too much pressure is applied.
Too many assignments writing the report
while men do the science.
Subsequent summers told, *Go over there.*
Do that instead, on construction sites.

Summer before grad year,
Grace applies to Service Canada
on a whim, nails the interview.
Her first day she feels
clouds of condescension dissipate,
an unfamiliar tingle, respect,
creeps into her work days.
She wonders if this is Utopia,
female energy flourishing,
a place where her opinions matter.
Her skill appreciated.

Grace graduates with a degree
she no longer intends to use.
The choice made easy
knowing no gender truce in sight
on the Engineering battlefield.

Former female colleagues confirm
inequities unlikely to change.
More opportunities exist in civil
service where she remains valued.

A Confidence Killer
for Batool Maallah

Confidence killer
Out of school
Virus twice
In Grade 10 & 11
Down, not out, in 12

Edge of Eighteen
for David Morales

If it's possible for someone 17
to distinguish between love
and infatuation, it will be David.

A capital 'R' Romantic
with cloud of dark hair,
he's in love with Love itself.

David sinks into a soft, white
leather chair to ponder
why a Grade 12 proclamation

of fidelity, sealed with library kiss,
did not kindle a lasting flame.
There's a reason "Jesse's Girl"

remains in radio rotation.
The song's unrequited scenario
repeats itself through generations—

the longing for a friend's fun-
loving girl. If she becomes
available, will she feel the same,

or will she let you down easy
by being too busy with a job,
and extracurricular curling?

David believes this problem is surmountable.
If two people are meant for each other,
time apart is but a blip, a sweetener.

Art school in Montreal next fall,
a small segment on a forever timeline.
But some people are all-or-nothing,

uncomfortable with murky greys,
leaving painters like David
to experiment with a palette

of other cities, and people
who enjoy process
as much as end product.

Eva Christensen
Oktoberfest
2020

Watercolour on paper
16 x 20 inches
Private Collection

**Sitting Outside a Bank Kiosk,
Embarrassing Money in My Hand**
for Keegan Burgess

Problems instantly shrink
when you meet a destitute man
outside a bank machine kiosk.

Just out of high school,
the irony of location
is not lost on Keegan.

Injured at one time,
this man sings with
the intensity of nothing left.

He was prescribed opiate relief,
and left. No follow up,
no refills for relief.

Desperate men grasp
desperate measures, demand Oxy
from pharmacists with nothing but

threats they can't back up.
After incarceration
without treatment,

all that remains
is a beat-up guitar,
the pain, and

a Green-to-the-World student
to sit beside him, listening
while he sings.

Three is a Magical Number
for Justine Walker

Parents teach children numbers
represent infinite possibility.
Count higher. Reach further.

Stretch your imagination.
Still, understanding atrophies
as we age. Searching stops,

convinced love has one shape.
After marrying her husband,
Justine learns the world is made for two.

Then their love expands,
enfolding a third.
A polyamorous triangle forms.

If love is strong, these bonds
will not break. Yet outdated laws
prevent pride of recognition.

Despite the obstacles,
they will spiritually affirm,
commit in globetrotting fashion,

where marriage accepts multiples.
Their children understand,
emotional math is simple

with acceptance.
Love is a tradition
but not traditional.

Advocacy is Love
for Shelley Petit

You could wake up disabled
one day. At any moment.
Debilitating diseases don't discriminate.

Imagine never attending school,
a concert, or sharing a first kiss.
These people exist. Everywhere.

Shelley believes she's lucky.
She had those experiences.
These days, babies are born
with her acquired condition—

Multiple Chemical Sensitivity
(MCS). 500 chemicals flowing
through an umbilical in utero.

Shelley had a fulfilling career,
15 years a teacher,
21 a Girl Guide leader.

One afternoon she woke
on a stretcher, staring
at her moldy classroom ceiling,
unable to breathe, beside

the janitor's chemical closet.
Please welcome to the stage
her new lead actor, Toxic TILT.

12 years prior, stage is set.
Detergent-induced headaches
become migraines,
evolve into anaphylaxis.

The antithesis of superpower,
she cringes from minute scents,
most times tasting them
prior to olfactory identification.

Slurring speech, she walks circles,
loses balance—ashes, ashes,
Shelley falls down—from
our collective chemical romance.

Homebound, she sheds
friends—those surprised by
the work it takes to accommodate.

She dons awkward ceramic masks
to filter out fragrances,
requires scentless visitations.

She does the math of loss.
If 90% of old life is gone,
write 3 letters to 2 daughters
and 1 mother, add 1 bottle
of pills, plus 1 bottle of wine.
Result: end of living nightmare.

But Fate intervenes.
Her partner's persistence
bucks trend of MCS spouses
decamping in divorce.

When strength and time permit,
Shelley now answers
the call to advocate.

She knows support
can save a life
in more ways than one.

Turbo Chargers for Dummies
for Alyson Samson

A turbo-charged engine sounds cool,
until it requires repair. *A Juke*
is a joke, the dealership says.
Two days tops, they say.

Then a week. Because...you know,
Parts Suppliers. *Eye roll.*
Then the last bolt...somehow
sends a wrench through

the windshield. Another week.
Okay. Fine. Renovating a house.
Hunker down. Get that job done.
Ready, again, Miss. No joke.

We'll see. Three-hour trek.
Visit family. Halfway there.
Heat gauge begins a dance,
syncs with odometer. Steady rise.

Dear, desolate highway gods,
let me make it. The hood smokes
in reply. Alyson has no offering.
Flames shoot from the edges—

race car in a cartoon. Speed dial
dealership. Shocked. Tow truck sent.
Rental returned. Parental unit
to the rescue with questions,

and Alyson a journalist without answers.
Told coolant line cut without malice,
all roads lead to Juke as training-day
guinea pig in search of a Red Seal.

First Sip
for Hai Vu

The first sip of love,
in-person or online,
leaves you drunk,
wanting more.

Little experience equals great
intoxication when a girl
chooses you for her sugar
daddy in a chat room

Quick survey of Romance classics
draws blossoming emotions
into the Tunnel of Love,
not knowing the first time through

it's riddled with spikes.
You pour out your heart,
she collects the blood.
You pay for her groceries

to help break bondage
to a domineering ex.
Offer free advice,
she should move

back in with her mother,
not knowing that reality either.
When she writes, *I love you*,
asks to be exclusive,

you send gifts
like any doting boyfriend.
Offer financial support
sight unseen.

Friends smell a scam,
you only smell roses.
The lonely computer programmer
longing for connection.

Together you create
consensual myth,
an obsession no different
than the controlling lover.

In the end,
it's an ideal fiction,
like everything you've read.
A pedestal for untested hearts.

Eva Christensen
Leave a Light On
2022

Watercolour and gouache on paper
8 x 10 inches

Serendipitous Holly
for Laurie McKenna Dacres

I

Friends appear in life for many reasons.
Long, or short-term; human, or animal.

Laurie's empty nest: two grown boys,
her Golden buddy Marley deceased.

Husband Rick's Cancer diagnosis,
near pandemic's start, creates

isolating conditions akin to penguin
research at the South Pole.

His Cancer is the insistent type,
won't cause death,

won't go away either.
Immunocompromised,

Rick and Laurie risk possible infection,
celebrate youngest son's engagement.

Later, they hold masked breath—
are told someone had COVID.

II

Son and fiancé want a dog.
Both are allergic.

They find a local breeder,
hypoallergenic Labradoodles,

get waitlisted.
Laurie follows the process,

hides the acute pain
caused by four-legged absence.

Then news of buyers backing out
as breeder drives pups

to new Fredericton homes.
Laurie knows training will be

a solitary task while Rick recovers
from chemo. Maybe this is

the cure for her loneliness.
Doubts dispel in a parking lot

without a name, or kibble, in mind.
Rick soon returns to golf greens.

Laurie walks wooded paths
once more, with Holly.

Regal Perseverance
for Sandi McKessock

In Green Village gardens,
Sandi sees a Monarch emerge
without working wings.

Taking tentative first steps,
the butterfly pauses—shudders,
knows something is wrong.

An August vacation in Mexico
not in this butterfly's cards.
Each day, doting staff

deposit her in different
raised garden vistas
to stimulate her senses,

discover milkweed
as home for final
contribution to species.

Sandi sees perseverance
personified, not just fleeting
beauty, as Miss Monarch tiptoes

through short-lived days
determined to live
life until it ends.

Pay Attention to the Signs
for Kathleen Boland

No guide exists to find your match,
yet gurus make such claims.
Don't dip into the workmate pool,
best trust in Cupid's aim.

This maxim's true for Air Force work,
day-in, day-out's the same.
The private and the workplace, brought
together, leads to shame.

Still, Kathleen has prophetic dreams,
of kissing work friend Mike.
She asks him on a movie date
to see if sparks alight.

Her manifested kiss ensues,
the power of a dream come true.

Scissors Required
for Caroline Theriault-Parker

At the terminus of a relationship,
a final awkward knot
needs to be snipped,
so frayed feelings cease.

Caroline never lost someone close
to anything other than death,
or a job. But a day of reckoning
with a close friend is coming

since casual, comfortable visits
degraded to an infrequent, back
and forth, snail mail campaign
designed to give distance

to unyielding advice.
Neither fitting, nor welcome.
Convinced Caroline's husband
can cure his chronic, post-

military anxiety and pain,
her friend draws a line
in desert sands, claims healing
trauma reduces anxiety,

which, in turn, shrinks inflammation.
Costly, experimental cures, her panacea
for a prismatic spectrum of problems.
Such suggestions imply resources

only available to the oblivious
upper echelon, those who feel
free to SHOUT from social media
platforms. Last letter sent

weeks ago. No lover of conflict,
Caroline prefers diplomacy,
realizes with any battle
there must be a final stand,

a cord must be cut.
Still, she wishes
it could be someone else
holding the scissors.

No Obligations
for Charles McAllister

Take it Easy is more than
a pop song to Charles. It is
3 minutes of harmonious carbon
containing the diamond—
Don't let the sound of your
own wheels drive you crazy.

Legs pumping pedals
creates meditative motion,
a rhythmic, rushing hiss replaces
thoughts of broken bonds.
Encumbered intimacies fade.
In the right gear—Nirvana.

Achievable alone, or in peloton.
Cyclists must trust the bum in front.
Draft the wrong rider,
become disastrously entangled.

Twelve years post heart attack,
Charles appreciates new camaraderie,
coffee and beer at mid-points.
No longer keeps score.

At a certain point on a ride,
cycling takes control,
becomes like walking.
Breathe in mistakes, exhale
them into the slipstream.

Let stat-obsessed youth count
kilometers and calories.
Charles is just along for the ride.

Eva Christensen
Light of the Moon
2020

Pen and watercolour on illustration board
9 x 12 inches
Private Collection

Depends on the Day
for Kathy Warren

Kathy steps into the Death Zone
for the first time 10 years ago
when her husband dies of Cancer.

Followed by her mother—Cancer,
Four best friends—Cancer,
and her dog—The Big C.

After the second friend passes,
word gets around, it's bad luck
befriending Kathy.

No doubt lessons to be learned,
as the witness. Better closure
by sitting vigil. An opportunity

to watch them leave.
A feeling of love, unspoken,
when the eyes close.

A bigger presence beyond
makes Kathy unafraid
to live in the moment

when another friend confides
that their relationship is worth
every possibly-traitorous cell.

Replacement Drummer Boy
for Duncan Allen

On the way to a Dieppe elementary school,
Duncan wonders how far someone should go
to help a friend, or a friend's mother.

The mother in question, is ready
to conduct an orchestra of six-year-olds
without a rhythm section.

Both bass and drummer out sick,
university son is hornswoggled to play bass,
then tasked to find a drummer.

Duncan agrees to help
in their hour of humiliating need.
Thrust into a gold-buttoned navy blazer,

he's ushered onto gymnasium stage
amidst a sea of sweaty hands
fumbling with recorders.

Nightmares born of recent
adolescent anxiety return.
Duncan remembers he doesn't read

sheet music, doesn't know
what song he is about to play.
Without music teacher's fluttery hand,

he wouldn't even know the tempo
required to punch through
a wall of off-key toots.

It's over before he can break a sweat.
Duncan takes a bow, not knowing
what is worth the standing ovation.

Childhood Monsters
for Ulfr Skogr

Ulfr's origin story
befits a dark hero.
Icelandic for wolf god,
she grows up in Saint John,
drug-addicted criminal
for a step-father.

Five-year-old Ulfr's toddler years
a revolving door in which she holds
her mother's hand each time
she suffers abuse, emotional
and physical. They leave—
are coaxed back by mother-in-law
money. The final time, Ulfr's future
college tuition the dangling carrot
enticing them back.

A typical Daddy-Daughter Day
includes a drive into the woods
with his friends to blow up a car.
The horrible sound still audible
when she hears a balloon pop.

Age 8, step-dad dies
in motorcycle accident,
leaves little Ulfr confused
about their mutual legacy.
His mother happily colours
in the blanks, recasts her son
as hero to idolize, not despise.
Ulfr still has doubts
as she plays the grief doll
on which others project.

***

Confused anger the new normal,
at age 12. Ulfr finds friendship
with charismatic teen. Someone
older, cooler, who decides
to help with her undiagnosed
Dissociative Identity Disorder
by labelling it Demonic Possession.

Ulfr is an atheist who likes a boy.
To keep her close, the teen saviour
decides to date this boy,
collects six other tweens,
proselytizes about a vengeful God
ready to hurt on a whim
without her claustrophobic protection.

As control increases, Ulfr becomes
uncomfortable, backs away.
Teen leader calls her bluff,
locks herself in an old building.
Stabs own leg with a pencil,
claims God will continue
to hurt her if Ulfr leaves.
An act against the older girl,
is in defiance of God, and
God loves to return a favour.

Manipulation continues.
Possession passion plays end
in more self-abuse, until Ulfr
understands cult of personality.

I Am Legacy
for Ella Hicks

For young dancers,
the rehearsal room
becomes second home.

Over time, those four walls
offer carefully choreographed
sanctuary six days a week.

Coach becomes both
mentor and friend.
She is sculptor. I am clay.

When coach retires
no one fills her empty shoes.
Should my years of practice,

and passion retire too?
Could I beat a new drum?
No, I am legacy.

Hers. My own.
Love of expression may change,
it never dies.

Taken root in young hearts,
freedom of movement,
body as art, a continuum.

Dumb Near Death Experience
for James Cormier

A high school play travels to England.
The scintillating subject: Canadian teens.

Five shows in two weeks. Too much
free time, too many hormones.

The group tours Bath, Wales, Norwich,
but it's in a London Tube station

where young James nearly meets
his dramatic and untimely end.

Fooling around with friends
on the noisy platform, he doesn't

feel the subtle air pressure shift, hear
the suction sound of brakes applied

as the hurtling underground train arrives.
Standing within inches of platform's edge,

his arm raised to hail his fellow thespians,
an elbow extends over the threshold,

is suddenly struck by the incoming train.
James spins like a top with nary a scratch,

avoiding certain death, and a phone call to family
informing them of the dumb way their boy died.

Eva Christensen
Brewbaker's
2021

Watercolour on paper
9 x 12 inches

Two Contradictions
for Jamie Robichaud

Even though they're adults,
I really miss my kids
since moving from Bathurst
to Fredericton for work.

I know my 20-something sons
are just hours away,
daughter in Newfoundland,
but to admit I miss them
might make their skin crawl.
Like asking for a kidney.

Getting sentimental
might contradict
my tattooed linebacker
do-as-I-say appearance.
Are they ready to know
I love them that much,
from a distance?

The boys balk at sleepovers
in my bachelor apartment
which contradicts their habit
of crashing on friends' futons.

Knocking on Tavern Doors
for Brent Buchanan

Brent struggles to focus,
teeters in front of thousands,
as emcee for Canada Day
celebrations in Officer's Square.

Well-past pleasant buzz, he drops
F-bomb adjectives like articles
as he introduces each entertainer.
That's where the memory ends,

until every embarrassing anecdote
is recounted by his boss at CKHJ
the next day at work. Hungover,
but happy to not hear,

clean out your desk.
A close shave, no worries,
all systems status quo. Drink
until 3 AM, on air at 5 AM.

Sign off at 10, wait for tavern
to open. Drink until close.
Finish up at home, alone,
family asleep hours ago.

Rinse. Repeat. Until New Year's Eve,
2014. Brent self-produces a show,
figures a few whiskies won't hurt.
Until a few becomes

telling everyone to fuck off
before the entertainment begins.
New Year's Day, he's unable to think
beyond leaving town

for the wasted anonymity of Toronto
streets—where the addiction began
in '87. A hotel bellhop boozing
on breaks, then through broadcast school,

into his current career. Or suicide.
A hamster can't see how to
stop the wheel while on it.
Sometimes it needs to be told,

it doesn't have to live
like an out-of-control train
headed toward an early grave.
With support from a family

living like roommates: wife
who's never known him sober;
daughter who witnessed him
in handcuffs, arrested for DUI;

a toddler too young to understand,
Brent chooses to change lanes,
take the road to recovery
no matter what it might reveal.

After initial setbacks, Brent celebrates
every October 2nd, his sober-versary.
Refocuses obsessive tendencies
into entrepreneurship,

opens a tattoo studio.
Starts an industry expo.
Becomes curator of permanent,
and meaningful connection.

Cool Teen Maggie
for Maggie Cronin

Working at summer day camp
for theatrical pre-teens, a challenge
Maggie takes on with gusto.

Another challenge—lack of
indoor plumbing at the Coach House,
home of the Calithumpians.

Each time a child must
answer the call of nature,
Maggie escorts them

to the rented Port-A-Potty.
On one such trip, a little girl asks,
Where do babies come from?

Maggie is horrified,
having only vague notions herself.
She responds that it's a question

best answered by a mom and dad.
Undeterred, the child asks,
Can two women have a baby?

A 9-year-old boy notices
Maggie's cheeks change colour,
Red apples to purple plums.

He confidently answers,
Yeah. There's strap-on stuff.
Maggie remains mum,

quickly returns them
to preferred tasks
before things escalate

into playground Sex Ed. class.
She tells the older counsellors.
Rookie mistake. This is the stuff

sticky nicknames are made of.
Cool Teen Maggie, they laugh. Ask her
the questions you can't ask your parents.

Never Drank the Kool Aid
for John Ackerson

The truth is out there.
Alternative social media. Piece it together. I did.
BitChute. Rumble. Odysee. Substack. They—
the wealthy. Central Bank. Orchestrating mass
genocide under our noses. Worse than the
Holocaust. Digital currency control. Farming
rules. Carbon tax. Spike Proteins. Vaccinated
kids. Only a few years to live. Big Pharma.
Maintenance drugs. Rich get richer from death
of poor. No grey areas. Cut and dry.
It's happening. The Media. Don't listen to CBC.
Lies to control. Do your own research.
Then it all makes sense.

Love is a bungee cord
for Diana Smith

it stretches and stretches
but never breaks.

Even after Diana's thankless attempts
to get her daughter addiction treatment.

Even after she desperately prays to God,
whether to sell out her own daughter.

Even after a cup of tea and cigarette
at Molly's to help clear her mind.

Even after a Buddhist Monk takes her on
a four-day prayer walk, talking to trees.

Even after Diana finally decides
to alert social services.

Even after her flesh and blood disowns her,
will not permit access to her grandbabies.

Eva Christensen
Freddy the Nude Dude
2020

Pen and watercolour on illustration board
9 x 12 inches

Grief is a Gift
for Vanessa Diosa

In a bedroom, the daughter hides,
prays to an impotent God,
If you can't kill her pain,
please take her away.

The mother wonders why
her brooding 14-year-old hates her,
spends days, weeks, months alone
in her room, avoiding her Cancerous mother.

Both are changing inside new cocoons.
Mother understands she will not emerge,
worries what type of person will erupt
from daughter's adolescent chrysalis.

Nothing sinister occurs.
Caring thoughts in infancy.
Vocabulary slow to subsume
concerns with pretty things.

In hospital, mother accepts
thoughtful staff's money
to get her nails done, but she
is beyond such fleeting frivolity.

A daughter's smile, the last item
a mother wants to purchase.
She receives it by gifting the cash
for daughter's desired dress.

Selflessness tears Vanessa's shroud.
Nothing compares to a mother's love.
Guilt and grief lead back to that smile,
the gift repaid.

A mother continues giving
in death. Grief is a gift,
transformed into joy by time.
Every star can wink,

I'm here. White butterflies
can congregate, lilt
amidst sadness—surrogates
for missing mothers' arms.

Lines that Heal
for Elizabeth Saunders

There I am, living
with my grandmother in Montreal,
nursing a broken heart.

The goal:
form a new chrysalis,
crawl out of my head,

with a transmogrified heart,
do something for myself.
Enroll in a figure drawing class.

One-minute, 10-minute poses,
no time to think
precious thoughts of Picasso.

Just get some lines down.
Remember the fearlessness
of childhood creation, when lines

and curves can be anything
you claim they are.
Thick, heavy marks express

masculine, soft curves
denote feminine freedom—
the winding roads we follow

that return us
to family, to Art.
To heal.

Immigration Steps for Newlyweds in the Time of COVID
for Neline De Villiers

Charles' love language is touch.
His wife, Neline, bought him
a bracelet connected to wifi.

When pressed, vibrations
are sent to its companion device
worn by a loved one.

This is how the newlyweds
express routine affection
over 12,000 kilometres apart.

***

Neline's parents emigrate
from South Africa to Fredericton in 2018.
Daughter to follow, post Physics degree,

with college boyfriend Charles.
But surprising no one,
they get engaged in 2019,

marry in January 2020. In June,
Charles' mother dies from Cancer,
at home surrounded by loved ones.

August arrives.
Neline must leave South Africa
to continue studies in Canada.

Easily done with her permanent
residency visa—a visitor visa
not as easily obtained for Charles,

a suspicious South African
computer scientist, who might
deliver a new COVID variant,

or seize the illogical opportunity
to remain in New Brunswick illegally
once it expires.

***

Missed occasions for celebration
cause the couple to create
new rituals. Traveling the world

becomes a necessity born of desire
to engage the 5 senses of the one
to whom you've dedicated your life.

South Africa.
Ireland.
Spain.

Cupid places pins on the map
of this unconventional relationship
that refuses to let immigration

bureaucracy dictate
separation
from soulmate.

Pissing into the Abyss
for Chuck Bowie

Being an international man of mystery
provides highs and lows. One moment
you are on a mission for the World Bank,
improving the Romanian Public Service,
the next, you almost meet your maker
while emptying your bladder.

Bucharest, city of intrigue, known for
Ceausescu's economy-swallowing palace,
and open-air drinking establishments.
One month in, Chuck and his boss
go out for a much-needed night on the town
with local colleagues. Drinks flow
while colleagues relate their amazing stories.

Bladder at capacity,
Chuck excuses himself,
wobbles away from their table,
is greeted by a miniature man
asking for 500 lei to enter the toilet.
Indignant, Chuck squabbles,
postpones the call of nature,
complains to his companions,
gobsmacked that peeing
requires monetary transaction.

Boss laughs, falls off his chair.
Chuck, how much is 500 lei?
With inebriated mental math
he calculates it to be 5 cents.
A colleague shakes his head,
I told you so! You pay to pee.

Chuck shuffles back to the pissoir,
gives the attendant 5 dollars in lei,
steps through the door
into pitch blackness.
He begins to urinate.
Something isn't right.
There's no splash.
No sound.

He leans back,
unnerved,
opens the door,
letting in some light,
looks at his feet
on the edge
of an abyss.

A Moment of Impact
for Emily Clancy

When you are 12, you bike
everywhere—to meet friends,
explore, escape the stress
of coexisting with family.

Emily crests the top of a huge
hill on her purple bicycle,
a feat worthy of celebratory rest.
She takes a moment,

soaks in the day,
listens to locusts
hum in the heat,
prepares to leisurely cruise

down the other side.
The reward of wind
turns hair aerodynamic.
Then it hits her!

Emily squeezes her brakes,
looks down, red welt forms
on her chest, dead bee
lies between her wheels.

The fuzzy fear of another
impact leads shaky girl
to walk away from her bicycle.
Walk everywhere from now on.

Eva Christensen
Up and Down the Boulevard
2022

Watercolour on paper
16 x 20 inches

Fourth Night Fright
for Jasmine Michel

Jasmine tags along to enjoy
final Folly Fest festivities
while her partner prepares
pizza for partying people.

Demand for Milda's menu so high
you'd swear it was cannabis.
Jasmine is soon conscripted,
assisting in food truck frenzy.

Four nights they camp,
a tent atop old plywood,
bathed in the aromas
of wet earth and cooking oils.

Night Four, exhausted,
they startle awake.
A constant sound near
their heads. Odd rhythmic

breathing like snoring.
They step outside.
All is silent, except those
who party until bitter end.

Jasmine and her beau lay
back down. Weird sound
becomes white noise.
In the hangover morning,

packing begins.
Board is lifted,
shedding light on source
of surreptitious sound.

A nest of blind baby mice
mewl, mother off to forage.
No time to linger,
lick labour's wounds.

Facing West
for Sebastián Salas

It's difficult to come out as lonely,
even harder than coming out gay
in a family-centric city
where being single, or childless,
is mistaken as social disease.

There is no medication
for loneliness. The cure
is people. Lots of people,
different stories to share.
A city's lifeblood is diversity,

its ability to seamlessly flow,
connect citizens and culture.
Fredericton is a great place
for families to grow up,
grow old in suburban bubbles,

not for outgoing Latin singles
searching for connection,
those who crave vibrancy,
variety, doors that remain open
to unannounced guests.

Sebastian believes in social capital,
is frustrated by its recession
in Fredericton. For 13 years
he created occasions to gather,
ended up preacher to the converted.

Don't misunderstand,
a congregation is a blessing.
You can feel loved in a place
and still feel left behind.

Sebastian is detaching
from New Brunswick's capital.
Unmotivated by ownership,
he left his job. Sold his house.
Moved to an apartment.
Preparation for flexible consultant life.

Pandemic's end created inward
complacency, self-contained
satisfaction—not open doors.
Reluctantly, Sebastian closes his.
On Sunday afternoons, he faces west

shuts his eyes, enters a portal
between past and future.
Reconnects with passions,
family gatherings, sunsets
over the Pacific.

This is when he vows to return to Peru,
without patriotic intentions,
care for beloved aging parents.
A simple mission now—to seek comfort
in a place that will always feel like home.

Do young artists bloom
for Riker Nelligan

in solitary, cultivated soil
behind white picket fences
with terriers and tree houses?

Or do they sprout from dust
at the bottoms of traveling shoes?
Depth of roots determined

by flexible parental occupations.
Riker's father, a healthcare worker
his unique skills in demand.

Four Canadian provinces, and
two stints in Ireland before age 12.
The constant, his father's arms.

Comfort of a tattooed embrace.
Silent symbology imprints line art
lullabies on his malleable mind.

Remember This
for Mark McKelvie

When life is wild,
sometimes you need
nice people to remind you
of what you already have.

Mark and his young family live
the life required of a med student.
Medical degree in Newfoundland,
hospital rotations in Woodstock, N.B.,
and wife's hometown, Truro, N.S.
Off again to Kingston, Ontario, to specialize,
family medicine and public health.

Passing through the Drive-Through Province,
Google suggests dining in Fredericton.
Isaac's Way. With two toddlers in tow,
public meals are always an adventure.
Dreading the all-night drive ahead,
Mark eats, deals with daddy demands.

They are about to leave
when two ladies at a nearby table
tell him he has a lovely family,
Enjoy it. This is the time of your life.

After two years in Kingston,
a job opportunity arises
in Fredericton. Interest piqued,
Mark and his wife reflect
on 12 weeks in Woodstock—
Saturday morning drives
to Boyce Farmer's Market for steak,
blue cheese, and a bottle of wine
with their names on it. For use
when kids finally fall asleep.

Jesus and the Bull Moose
for Mike Romard

During my Grade 12 English exam,
Mr. Kemp stalked aisles of desks,
a hunter surveying his territory,
searching for the weakest prey.

Earlier in the semester, Catherine
and I swore to boycott his class
if presented with more dead-animal-
as-religious-allegory literature.

We solidified this stance
after being force-fed
Alden Nowlan's "The Bull Moose."
That was it.

Lapsed Catholics are blurry
at best on Resurrection details.
I asked Mr. Kemp how accurate
Jesus Christ Superstar was

compared to the Bible.
A musical fan, this was how
I'd tackle the analysis.
He intoned from on high,

Just write what I said in class.
Luckily, the English Lit boycott
died prematurely, permitting
another miraculous resurrection.

For me, exams were something
to glance at, and be gone— the only
races I could count on winning.
I raised my hand, left the echoey gym.

Eva Christensen
*View of the Playhouse
on a Chilly Evening in May*
2020

Ink and watercolour on illustration board
9 x 12 inches

Futures in Bloom
for Ming Lin

A milestone in a colleague's life
can often trigger a cognitive leap
into a selfsame future scenario.

One career in its infancy, while
another ages out into retirement.
At 24, Ming wonders what the end

of a life in landscape architecture
will mean in 40 years. Achievement
in his field? A balanced, fulfilled life?

Questions impossible to answer
at the outset, but not frivolous.
Seeds from which futures bloom.

Difficult Colours
for Noah Trethewey

Mottled brilliance of chameleon leaves,
a concert audience on the horizon,
120 km/h on the crest of a highway hill.
My son loves fall colors.

Brittle gutter leaves under my feet
are your idiotic face, belly mom.
Always in my head, you
ignore me, starve me, lock me
in the bathroom with my brother
to play with our feces.
No light, we grow scrubby
like pesky ground cover
ripped from perfect lawns.

He hates crackers, bread,
flat food that can slide under a door.
Repeats odd sounds, can't stop
talking about butt holes, poop.

My ugly face is yours.
Don't take my picture.
I'm not worth remembering.
I'm glad these leaves are dead.
I wish I was dead. Stupid idiot.
Should kill myself.

School-approved, traffic light symbolism:
green calm, yellow anxious, red rage,
to aid articulation. Only works with kids
who get the point of self-
regulation in society.

Attachment crinkles to impermanence.
Delayed traffic patterns of boys
born into locked kennels. Now forever mine,
he paddles to stay afloat in a green calm sea
with yellow anxious sunset, red rage
night sky. The forgotten child,
awestruck by a landscape.

Do You Want to Lean on Me?
for Hilary Swan

Hilary is drawn to Stephen.
Best friends and neighbours
on St. John Street for three years
of kayak and camping trips,
Saturdays at The Market.
She accepts romance will never happen,
settles for soul mate. Perhaps
their children, with other,
future spouses, will be best
friends as well. Stephen decides

to move. Halifax. He'll stay in touch,
of course. Three days prior to move,
arms touch on a couch.
She thinks, *That's weird.*
He asks, *Do you want to lean on me?*
Hearts race. A long-time-coming kiss.
When he moves, letters, and
every-third-weekend alternating
visits begin. A year later
he returns to Heaven in Devon.

Nearly Dead Drew, Rural Houdini
for Drew Gilbert

Near Death Experience #1

Prevailing wisdom states
face your fears to conquer them.
Drew isn't a good swimmer,

but if the day calls for swimming,
he'll be the first one wet.
Petitcodiac kids know how

to wring every drop of fun
from rural life. On hot summer days,
they descend on Pollett River

for cliff diving at Gibson Falls.
Most popular platform—20 feet
above the 35-foot plunge pool.

Drew and his buddies egg each other
on to greater heights. The last diver
shaken by his 75-foot drop.

To turn it down a notch, friends
decide to swim upriver, splash around
in current-created pools.

Sun begins to set, they swim
back to entry point. Drew is thin.
His makeshift strokes

drain his batteries, his legs
sink like lead weights.
Companions already on shore,

Drew feels himself go under.
With last gasp, he screams,
Not gonna make it!

Exhausted, he sinks—
unable to break surface tension,
or hit the bottom and shoot up.

Drew is certain he'll drown,
feels it happening,
when hands grab him,

push him to the surface.
Grateful the friend who heard him
is a strong swimmer.

Flabbergasted by being saved,
Drew swims back to shore,
shakes it off, jumps back in.

***

Near Death Experience #2

Craig owns a 35-foot sailboat,
needs to sail it from St. Andrew's
to Fredericton. Drew is game to learn.

Near Pocologan, the bolt rope comes
unhooked from the mast. Craig
concedes the need for the engine.

But not the new old salt, Drew,
now self-proclaimed captain, who offers
to rise, suspended in bosun's chair.

1 foot. 10 feet. 15 feet.
At 20 feet above the deck,
you can see the whole boat

on the ocean, and it's beautiful.
Serenity arrives, rocking 10 feet
side-to-side in the Bay of Fundy.

Slow to Develop
for Joni Leger

Relationships can be
like Polaroid photographs—
slow to develop. Murky.

Two single parents, working
at two different institutions
have little time

to play the dating game.
But play they must.
Neither Joni, nor Felipe, is willing

to succumb to hermetic solitude.
Research & Innovation conferences
become Joni's accessible chess board,

a Queen scanning academic
congregants for sparks from a King.
Her gaze finally lands upon Felipe.

Awash in collegial admiration,
Joni cannot gain access
to his inner circle.

Like bats, they flutter
inside the same sphere,
yet fail to find each other alone

until a Moncton conference.
Joni finds Felipe waiting
patiently for the podium.

She musters her courage.
Must see if she can kindle a flame.
He recognizers her,

they talk over tea,
he gives her his digits,
cell number on card,

intention of which, she fixates on
for months on end.
Was the number given for work,

or for a future rendezvous?
In the end, Joni decides
nearly three years is long enough

to discover if her interest is one-sided.
Another Christmas is about to pass
alone. She pulls out his card,

sends him an email expression
of her desire to date,
which pings his phone in Portugal.

Typically oblivious, Felipe
tells his sister, I think a girl
just asked me out.

That was 2018—
four year later,
Joni, Felipe, and their blended

brood couldn't imagine
her not having the courage
to follow her heart.

Eva Christensen
Thirty Minutes or Less
2021

Watercolour and gouache on paper
11 x 14 inches

After Images
for Seren Hearn

Best friend gone at 18,
epileptic seizure in his sleep.
At minor hockey, he took Seren
into his big, bear-hug embrace
making them siblings forever.
No one messed with his little sister.

5 months pass.

Father dies at 55,
pulmonary thrombosis from asbestos-
laden buildings at Base Gagetown.
Typical Military Dad raised
7 children on tough love tasks.
His filling lungs prevent seeing fruition.

Seren's memory shutter snaps 7 times.
Once each for: mother, 5 brothers, 1 sister.
No matter their love languages
she remembers to use the actual words.

Wet Nose Wake-up
for Ben Wolthers

Dads on their own do better
with their children au naturel.
In the elements with orange
canvas bell tent heirloom,
broken door flap zipper.

Ben's parents separate before
he turns 10. His favourite early
memories are of rustic camping
at the end of a long, muddy, logging
road in Martin's Head, NB.

The end of the desolate track
reveals a beautifully empty
gravel beach. A place to sit
with the quiet wisdom of
father, and Bay of Fundy.

One memorable trip, a classic
camping family—husband, wife,
large brown Lab, 2.5 kids—frolic
at the opposite end of the beach.
By evening they are gone.

Dad and Ben enjoy the ritual
tent set-up, campfire crackle,
and star gazing, before retiring
on the weight displacement trampoline
otherwise known as an air mattress.

In the middle of the night, Ben
wakes to a wet sniffing sound
by his ear. He reaches out
tentatively, feels matted fur,

whispers, *Dad! There's something
in the tent!* Fumbling for flashlight,
father reveals an enormous Chocolate
Lab, who proceeds to crawl
between them and go to sleep.
At dawn, the dog leaves

the tent to sit sadly on the beach.
When 10 o'clock rolls around,
so does its family. The familiar camper
lumbers down the beach. Brown dog
trots away, knowing faith is rewarded.

sidewalk running backs
for the Football Jersey Twins

they speed walk
situation doesn't matter
third and eight
fourth and long
twins constantly clad
in one of 32 colours
depending on the NFL news
paying no allegiance except
to a love of the game

each time you pass them,
acknowledge that you're
a lazy, car-bound slob, as they
pound the gridiron sidewalk
jersey arms pumping
smiles ever-present

they circumnavigate the city solo
twice a day as if repelled by magnets
creating the illusion of one man
with special teleportation powers
shimmying to headphone cheers

each twin feints right, then
left outside supermarkets
cradling 20-pound paper
bags of potatoes like pigskins
streaking to end zone
home on game days to dine
and draft tomorrow's team
onto their backs

Some Voodoo Juju
for Amy Floyd

Amy has a particular digital photo
buried on a memory card
from a trip to Africa in 2009.

Not unusual for a tourist
to capture exotic life events,
never to look back.

Some frozen moments
are so bizarre you cannot bear
to revisit them, nor delete.

With time to kill in Lome, Togo,
Amy and friends visit
the Akodessawa Fetish Market,

the world's largest congregation
of Juju practitioners and wholesalers.
After she haggles with a local con man

wanting 30 Canadian each to enter
the free market, the friends find their way
to a windowless, sand floor shed.

They witness a Juju ceremony performed
by the grandson of an absent priest.
Inside the dark structure, filled with animal

skulls, assorted paraphernalia from
the earth-based religion, he begins to chant,
rattle cowrie shells. A chained monkey

and raptor watch them intently.
The apprentice priest tosses the shells

to the floor like dice. Still miffed
about caving to the entry fee hustle,
Amy pulls out her camera,
takes a forbidden photo.

Promptly chastised, she leaves.
In Northern Ghana, she flicks though
photos from the market.

Finds the ceremony.
In it a woman,
fabric wrapped around

her chest, big necklace,
face painted white.
Not there before.

Thin Ice in Lewisporte, Nfld.
for Darroch White

Darroch's a student with the task,
in Principal Sniper's History class,
of getting the teacher's train off track
via verbal sparring match.

On winter morning walks to school,
Darroch sometimes plays The Fool.
A frozen pond near the schoolyard,
he slides on out to prove it's hard.

Fresh from trade school class in drafting
Darroch has everybody laughing.
Yells, *It's safe!* Stomps his boot.
Climbs back out. What a hoot!

Dutiful Darroch's clothes are soaked,
won't go home, sits down and hopes
Sniper won't kick him out the door
as water pools over the floor.

While handing back a prior test,
Sniper's shoes slap past his desk.
Looks around, *Where is this from?*
Scolds his friend, not the guilty one.

Boots off young man!, his request,
You've made a bloody awful mess!
Friend shakes his head, gets his sneakers,
does not argue with the speaker.

Sniper earned his nickname, honest,
from hall patrols, and smoky office.
Ciggy butts flicked 'cross the room,
gave all, but Darroch, sense of doom.

Eva Christensen
August Evening at Officer's Square
2020

Ink and watercolour
on illustration board
9 x 12 inches

Passion Begets
for Matt Carter

Dad records radio through thirty feet
of FM beats.

A boosted signal up from Maine.
A pain

to hear his favourite Celts
and Scots.

Agree we hate each other's tunes.
Soon,

I'm in high school, late at night,
headphones tight

tuned to Brave New Waves.
Save

my faves with Dad's old set-up.
What

do I see right in front of me?
He

looks back. No one wants
haunts,

yet behaviours can echo
in chromosomes.

Not Hard to Make a Difference
for Dawn DeCourcey

Girls need to be in school, not traded
for cattle at first menstruation. Girls—

a commodity. Unless someone gives
them a choice, there is no choice.

North America understands this, mostly.
It's not obvious to nomadic Masai men

of Kenya, who measure prosperity
by daughters they can trade

for cattle. Dawn sees this first-hand. Nine
years ago, upon retirement from teaching.

Meets young girl named Kilayo at impoverished
elementary feeder school in Mara Region.

Kilayo dreams of teaching. It doesn't seem possible.
Jump to 2022, and twelve fully-funded, female

high school graduates later, Dawn directs her vision
to help one girl at a time at Friends of Kilayo,

her newly registered non-profit. Its namesake,
finishes her degree. Early childhood education.

While *her* mother babysits the two children
Kilayo begat before she met the light of dawn.

Jason Anderson is a Date Night Excuse
for Jason Anderson

Date nights—a necessity for caregivers
who've almost exhausted all care.

I'm excited to share a new friend's act
at another friend's café. Coffee

and craft beer with my best friend
who's been weakened by listening

to her mother quickly forget
who her daughter is.

Macrame-held plants, and ghost
lights, are backdrop for Jason's

sweaty stage ethic. He works
a crowd ready to be held rapt

by details draped in melody.
Snoopy stamp and shaky signature

on a cathedral Christmas card,
so vivid it almost makes me cry.

Does make my wife smear
streaks in her foundation.

Troubadour nods to the poet
before beginning singalongs

to keep misty darkness at bay.
On cue, his strings break

into a tale of kindness: Sam
in overalls, goes out of his way,

gets gas for strange storytellers
on a West Texas highway.

Cop Killers Kill More than Cops
for Sarah Burns, In Memoriam

Fuck da police!
A counter-culture call to arms
meaning fuck-the-racist-
abuse-of-power-pieces-of-shit-police.

A powerful refrain that continues to run
unbidden in my anti-authoritarian brain.
Anger at society's resource-hoarding elite,
turned on those charged with our safety,

despite friends who chose badge careers.
Neighbours employed by governments
to enforce bylaws, maintain community safety
standards, during their work week.

Like Sarah—
mother of three school-aged sons.
All-around generous individual.
The type to instigate employee potlucks,
commiserate about a mutual past-
employer's Machiavellian machinations,
who donates her boys' used hockey gear
to your newly-adopted five-year-old.

A woman with a job, ambushed
by a bullet at 43. Two years into
her public service, staying late, providing
back-up for co-worker after night shift's end.

She responds to the improbable—
shots fired in Fredericton,
at an apartment complex
up the street from the summer
day camp where I dropped off
my son five minutes earlier—
her time of death.

A Prolonged Youth
for Darrell Mesheau, In Memoriam

The secret to prolonged youth
is not guarded by magicians.
Longevity is a trick of the mind,
easily-performed, if willing
to set aside world-weary,
know-it-all notions that clamp
our minds shut with age.

I feel an old fool
upon a return to university
at 23. I decide to try something
unexpected for an introvert
desperate for a new beginning.

The stage beckons
after watching a performance
including not just fresh-faced frosh,
but older community members
playing necessary character scenery.
Once welcomed backstage,
I gravitate to Darrell, the resident
Senior at home amongst Juniors.

He navigates archetypes,
real and imagined, first encountered
40 years prior, with skill and interest
in the fleeting and frivolous, and
those who take themselves a tad
too seriously in diversions.

Supportive and interested,
good friend and countryman,
he lends an ear, and his support,

appears with a chuckle, and all-
knowing smile. Darrell's is not
a one-time-only friendship.
When you encounter him in the wild,
he poses thoughtful questions,
and waits for the answers.

Eva Christensen
Spring at Head Hall
2021

Watercolour and gouache on paper
12 x 16 inches

Nacho Neighbour
for Jessica Wilcox and Ethan Shaddick

It's said the way to a man's heart
is through his stomach. But when
Jessica finally allows Ethan entry
to her home, it is his culinary skill

on courtly display. Jessica can't sleep.
His company a welcome distraction.
Ethan's self-styled nachos comfort
on a night not considered a date.

Next morning, Ethan meets Jessica's
mother for the first time despite
their families living a few houses
apart in Lincoln their entire lives.

Their stars first cross at Klub Khrome
when Ethan asks for a lift home.

Break a Leg, Not Both Arms
for Charlotte Pearn

Going to the splash park
should be fun in the sun
but beware of your surroundings
before you start to run.

Take for instance, Charlotte,
pumped for a day like this,
before she takes a step
she trips and breaks both wrists!

This Indian Woman Couldn't Possibly
for Gail Standingready

Childhood amnesia makes recollection spotty.
One of Gail's most treasured, real, memories,
a school nurse, gentle, and kind,
while she waits in line
for her Polio vaccine.

***

In 1983, 15-year-old Gail scans
her Social Services file after emancipation
from Province of Saskatchewan custody.
A child in care from infancy, she bounces
between foster and bio homes.

This Indian woman couldn't possibly
look after 11 children, it reads.
Big Brother Canada knows best.
Social workers descend with Sixties Scoops
for Gail and her 10 older Dakota siblings.

Her parents, Residential School Survivors,
once more badgered and belittled.
Her own brood legally kidnapped,
Gail's mother begins a never-ending
search for shelter at the bottom of bottles.

Gail leaves the southern Saskatchewan
courthouse euphoric on her emancipation day.
Happy to be free despite only owning
a shopping bag of clothes. Nowhere
to put them, she hitches to Ottawa,

finds her way into the federal civil service
by promising to attend school twice per week.

At 23, she moves to Fredericton. Works admin
to support her children, until that one *good*
memory reminds her she once had a dream.

***

Gail is living her dream, these past
15 years. A registered nurse,
she cares for long-term patients
at York Care Centre, where
she's known as gentle, and kind.

Heartache Revisited
for Amer El-Samman

Nobody wants to revisit heartbreak.
Rejection is painful, and the amount
of time it takes to become water off
a duck's back, is different for everyone.

Amer falls in love while living in London,
Ontario. A commensurate crush,
until the crush in question crushes Amer,
by offering her affection to someone else.

The London lady continues calling
the home Amer has made in Fredericton
with his bride, a mutual friend. Reminds
him of humiliation left behind.

Amer's depression, once more, does enfold,
asks his wife to put that friendship on hold.

Adversity Builds
for Bob Dewar

Before she dies from an auto accident,
Bob's mother tells her five sons,
Stick together, boys,
you might be all that you have.

In hospital that day, one floor below,
Bob's son is born. Prompts his mantra;
be calm in the face of adversity,
and there's a lot of adversity.

His grandfather fought in WWI,
came home to Campbellton,
opened Cash & Carry grocery chain.
Fed the region on credit

during Great Depression. Went bankrupt
when no one paid him back.
Business now infused in the blood,
Bob and his brothers become

successful entrepreneurs
(himself in the burger business).
Continue look out for each other
with interest.

Eva Christensen
Love This Town
2021

Watercolour on paper
14 x 18 inches

Orbiting Bodies & Celestial Remnants
for Nathaniel Brewer

Nathaniel is hyperactive. A student
at Fredericton High School, his teacher
unaware that by placing him near Michelle,

the proverbial calm centre of the universe,
two powerful opposing forces will
perpetually orbit each other's lives.

Friendship develops over Doors albums
via headphone intimacy. By Grade 11,
an official inseparable tandem exists.

Trips to see Michelle play soccer at college
in New Jersey with her parents eventually end.
Their orbits take five years to perigee again

in Fredericton, near the Paragon Cleaners.
Her, beginning a Masters in Kinesiology.
Nathaniel, recently leaving it.

***

Two earthbound bodies observe the night sky,
rogue campers in Fundy Park. A reprieve
from COVID claustrophobia.

On nights like this, they search
for Cassiopeia, their favourite constellation.
Visible whether together, or apart.

With their first child, a daughter, due
in January, everything becomes connected.
New year, new life, underneath ancient

supernova light of Cassiopeia A.
A new star is born. Positive repels
negative. In the end Nova remains.

Spoke Folk
for Judy Hawkins

Folks on Spokes,
it's no joke.
This exercise,
to Judy's surprise,
began in earnest
after career in guidance.
Thirty-five years.
counseling peers
Found biking
to her liking.
Cycled Ireland, Spain,
sun and rain.

Atop spokes,
with her beloved folk,
peddle Fredericton trails
Tuesdays without fail.
Midpoint stop for snack.
then turn back
Penniac, Keswick Ridge,
they love to cross the walking bridge
for coffee, muffins, weekly tales,
politics, and pints of ale.

Landscaper Hoodie
for Alejandra Paredes

Love at first blush is only cliché
until it happens to you. To say it aloud,
Alejandra knows, sounds stupid.
He cares because his eyes sparkle

with compassion. A perfect smile
reassures her she's gorgeous
in the morning. Little details,
like wild flowers for behind an ear,

a dog named Bella, her favourite
princess. Loves books and music,
never pushes. Yet gives her
vague final notice four weeks in.

He texts, *Not really a relationship guy*.
She'll keep his hoodie to remember him by.

Recalibration
for Ken Spragg

If things go according to plan, Ken will
step into the role he's currently creating
for himself—a popular writer, due to his
main character. A Communist fish
afloat in a Capitalist sea. Someone
out to spread doctrine of community
cooperation, kindness. Written by
Hadrian Ken Allen Vanguard.
When interview requests roll in, Ken
will legally become the pseudonym,
in name and outlook. Mother and father
now deceased, Ken takes stock of
what baggage to keep. No need for
father's ego and anger; to yell
at kids for laughing too loud. Unloved
by a Nazi-sympathizing Englishman
who preferred Arian-featured brother.
This understood, a synthesis occurs.
Mother the measure of virtue by which
Ken calibrates. He'll keep given names,
the meat between fresh bread.

The Point
for Luke van Reede van Oudtshoorn

In three nights on Hogan's Hill,
Luke learns N.B. forests are swamps
with trees that rip you apart.

Three days of practical navigation
training at CFB Gagetown, not-
sleeping under tarps in the rain.

But night is Luke's time to shine.
Scores two of two despite fireflies
feigning the points' artificial glow.

Eva Christensen
Three Little Ghosts
2021

Watercolour on paper
8 x 10 inches

RomCom Daze
for Molly Wilby

If life follows a script,
Molly's is a romance.
Self-declared romantic,
she likes to go and dance.

S-Club on Halloween,
Jude, a quiet hippie.
Molly Playboy Bunny,
glad that he seems groovy.

Jude's namesake song written
by beetle-headed Paul.
Her favourite song. Coincidence?
So quickly does she fall.

Of happiness in love,
she will never ever tire.
RomCom days continue,
Hallmark man beside her.

Chocolate Milk
for Hailey Dunphy

Hailey doesn't drink chocolate milk
anymore. Three years since
it last touched her lips. Four years

since a certain boy first opens
the tricky lid for her while she worked
at a gas station convenience store.

Like clockwork, the boy visits Hailey
on the job each month. Buys her
her favourite drink. Opens it.

They chat during consumer lulls,
his outrageous commentary causes
spontaneous snorts, occasional snot.

She is eighteen, and he is the first
boy she brings home to meet the parents,
and four intimidating Burnedoodles.

Hailey remembers good communication.
Except on weekends, as he lives
out of town, no cell coverage.

These 48-hour periods feel like weeks.
A year into their relationship,
an uncommunicative weekend turns

into 72 hours. Continues for five days.
Now at Greco, Hailey's sauce-covered
hands smear her smart phone

every time it rings, she hopes it's him.
On the sixth day, when it buzzes,
his mother responds, *Hailey, I'm sorry.*

ATV driver discovers him in his car, both wrecked
in a ditch. Off a remote road returning from work.
Cannabis consumption unofficial culprit.

All Answers Lie Within
for Lauren Laarik

If not a proper story,
it doesn't matter to Lauren.
To write is to attempt
an understanding of life.

As a child, she imagines
people reading her journal.
It influenced how she wrote,
self-consciously.

She thinks long term now.
Backstories. How we write
our own futures. Make
meaning without control.

Twin Flames from Dying Embers
for Caelia Sutton

Born with Spina Bifida,
Caelia lately learns
her mother never wanted her.

Why did it take so long?
Love looks different
to those mistreated from birth.

Raised under a loveless roof,
Cealia cannot gauge compassion
for herself, or others.

Submits to abusive relationships.
Is lucky to have escaped
alive. No time to learn

comfort in own skin,
consider her pansexuality,
when basic needs never met.

When a childhood friend re-
enters her life at a funeral,
familiarity washes over them,

like they've known each other,
previous incarnations.
This time, there is energy

to protect each other.
Learn to love, and be
loved in return.

Right & Wrong Raphael
for Nomaan

Before you book an Airbnb in Spain,
Nomaan advises that you ask for
a photo if your host is named Raphael.

You may be presented with multiple
Raphaels on the same intercom list,
at the same apartment complex.

If the first Raphael you ring
buzzes you in, opens his door shirtless,
rubs sleep crust from his eyes,

only speaks Spanish, and is terrible
at charades, he may misinterpret
your request to be shown to your room.

This Wrong Raphael might smile,
click his fingers, disappear
into his dark room to return with

a tissue packed with marijuana.
You might need to call the Right
Raphael, have him speak to Wrong

Raphael to discover Right Raphael
is in the same building. After Wrong
Raphael relays your location to him.

However, should you spend four days
in Valencia at a Physics conference,
and only meet the Right Raphael,

you will not bump into the Wrong
Raphael again, insisting
you take two joints this time.

Eva Christensen
The Tannery
2021

Watercolour on paper
18 x 24 inches
Private Collection

The Pain Cave
for Krista Steeves

Rowing attracts vulnerable people
grown steady on rocking boats.
As a child, Krista learns to forget pain,

a survivor of terrible sexual abuse.
Her only memories before age 12,
escape visits to grandparents,

the smell of their lilac bushes.
Digging clams. Scenes to draw upon
in The Pain Cave—what regatta rowers

call that peak time mid-race,
when thighs burn. You suck wind.
But on exit, exhilaration.

Permanent Marker
for Eddie Young

Attending a wedding,
belligerently drunk,
double fisting his wine,
Eddie falls down. *Kerplunk!*

A fetching young mother,
grabs a Sharpie, and friend,
then rolls Eddie over.
Holly's art time begins.

Soon after, she asks him,
Can you burn some CDs?
He shows up for the ruse,
makes the disc, never leaves.

A twenty-year see-saw,
four children to parent,
lived Food Bank conditions,
could barely pay rent.

Careers. A good home.
Now both can be proud.
Twenty years to the day,
now he says this aloud,

Becoming a parent
while still in your teens,
caused you to miss out
being wild and so free.

I promise you, Holly,
as a wave comes ashore,
if you'll have me, I'm here
for twenty years more.

The Mentor
for Ilkay Silk

She molds us all with an imperceptible touch. Egoless,
her un-staged wit and grace elicit devoted following.
We'll do anything for it—her smile, or laugh, of approval.

Poems written for the City of Fredericton

2021-2023

The Wolastoq River's Counsel

A river doesn't care
about boundaries. Persistence
gets it where it wants to go
no matter what's in its way.

A river acknowledges us
in passing,
could care less
if we disappear tomorrow.

A river is eternal optimist—
gravity holds it down,
pulls it forward, yet
it still shoots for the Moon.

A river is unattainable beauty.
We fall in love, get too close
try to tame it, name it, call it ours.

A river provides
to creatures great and small.
It cannot be owned,
lets us know when we get too close.

A river pushes back.
It is not a metaphor
for the mindless masculine march
toward vague destiny fixed to the horizon.

A river watches plagues
force us indoors—apart,
waits to welcome us back
from cages of our own construction
once we cure what we created.

A river whispers wisdom
in every tongue if we choose to listen.
It follows a logical arc,
Hard lines are man-made.

A river is feminine,
a natural occurrence of curves.
She leads by example.

A river is current,
never stagnant.
She defines
progress
balance
comfort.
Her counsel is considerate
with concern for all.

A Christmas Tree is Memory

Charlie Brown tosses his needle-less twig
near Snoopy's dazzling doghouse display.
His cast of Yuletide tormentors walk by
his ridiculed choice, wracked with guilt
from crippling Chuck's Christmas spirit.

No longer blinded by the bright
lights of empty consumerism,
children use furious-fast hands,
turn misguided angst against
the golden idol of excess,
transfer wealth to the poor,
restore faith in community
lifting the lowest branch up.

A Christmas tree is a brief reason
to downshift from our daily drive
toward pursuit of subsequent desires.
Chopped down in its prime,
the Christmas tree transforms—
becomes focal point for memories.

Nostalgia triggered by the scent of sap,
we drag dusty boxes from attics and basements
filled with poinsettia-ed paraphernalia.
Mutter curses untangling strings of lights
only to discover the whole strand dead
due to one burnt out mystery bulb.
Wrestle with whether it's worth
a painstaking search to replace it
or admit defeat—
purchase another to suffer
the same fate next year.

Maybe it is mothballed sentimentality
we smell, the reason tired parents,
jaded teens, and tantrum toddlers alike
gather around folded box flaps
marked "Tree Ornaments."
Each one a time capsule
delineating the best of times
in construction paper, macaroni,
Styrofoam, yarn, and finger paint.
Years guessed at and recalled
upon unpacking decorations
gifted to us in years when we grew
too busy to remember
our sons' and daughters',
mothers' and fathers',
passions and proclivities.

Oh, Tannenbaum!
Light our living room lives,
if only for a few weeks.
Be a healing evergreen heart,
the moment of respite required
to face a cold new year.

Eva Christensen
The Dip
2021

Watercolour on paper
12 x 16 inches

Winter Anthropology
after viewing Lindsey Mackay's "Winter Lake Skate"

Childhood winters are slightly different
in cities and villages.

In cities, moms and dads construct backyard arenas,
hope to lure unambitious Stojkos and Wickenheisers
from electronic cocoons within newly-amalgamated home offices.
Anything for a break to return to work,
earn enough to flood and light their lawns next season.

In villages, desperate moms and dads hire
heavy machinery, excavate ovals of rocky woodland
down to water table, prepare for the season
without temperate outdoor activities. Spare no expense.
Get wild sibling multiples outside, blow their stink off.

In cities, parents add Zamboni duty
to their list of surfaces requiring after-snowstorm scraping.
Calamity, should pre-teen pros pull precocious hamstrings.
Dad Dreams of arena roars now rest
upon uninterested shoulders of E-Sport enthusiasts.

In villages, parents purchase shovels and scoops.
When snow stops, they inform offspring—
ice doesn't clear itself once driveway is uncovered.
Hockey on lumps, and shell ice, as terrible as it sounds.

In cities, boys and girls rush inside
when rosy cheeks and tender feet begin to chafe,
as fingers get uncomfortably cold. Soothe
with hot chocolate and Internet.

In villages, kids stomp inside after dark
for any combination of the following reasons:
soaked in stew of sweat and melting snow,

concussion, or seeking first aid
to staunch a bleeding frenemy's wound.

Childhood winters, urban and rural,
each a little different, yet one thing is similar—
the family recreation budget keeps clans
together by providing time apart.

No One Chooses This

I – Homeless and Hopeless

No one chooses homelessness.
Just as no one chooses to be born with,
or acquire, disorders of the mind.

Nor is it a healthy person's choice to be
neglected and abused by those they trust,
people they never knew to fear.

Left one day without essential support
systems we take for granted—family,
jobs, friends. Gone, or never existed at all.

No one chooses to shelter—
if it can be called that—Shelter,
in a nylon tent on a riverbank.

Wind Chill minus 40,
possessions one gust away from
flight when occupant rises

on stiffened limbs to empty
irritated bladder which cannot heal
due to inadequate treatment options,

transportation to clinics, and
lack of, or inability to, work,
acquire a meal outside of stringent

community kitchen hours, insufficient
to ward off malnutrition, frostbite, depression.
Self-soothing options are available

for a price, should a day of successful
panhandling provide the choice
between escape, or full stomach.

II - 12 Neighbours

Bureaucratic t's are crossed, i's dotted.
Real social accommodation begins
one tiny house at a time.

Shifting a paradigm requires plenty of torque.
Poor circumstances lead to heavy losses.
When there is nothing left to lose

people don't pull up their bootstraps.
Rocky Balboa is a fiction. After suffering
innumerable defeats, you are defeated.

You find a bottle, a needle, some pills.
You do not get back up. Not without support.
Not without established systems that

understand everyone has value,
that therapeutic hours, and money,
must accompany ideology.

Can we call ourselves a "society,"
if we ignore our most vulnerable?
Look closer. We reflect each other.

We are in the same precarious boat
at the mercy of rolling rent increases, market
fluctuations, and bottom lines rising higher

and higher, locking more of us out
each year. Everyone deserves dignity,
a small, safe place to heal—

call home out of the cold.
We all need neighbours
to lend a hand now and then.

Post-Pandemic Echo

In my post-pandemic search for Wonder,
I wonder

if Wonder is possible any more.
The more

I look, the more I force "pre-" onto "post-."
Close-

fitting comparisons reduce the near
fear

of what's to come. Can I once more ignore
spores?

Stay clean without sanitizing in every space?
Face

friends and neighbours with a naked smile
while

muscle memory lifts atrophied lips,
flips

smiling eyes back to utilitarian sight.
Might

mouth return as key signal of mood,
attitude?

Is a visit with grandparents possible?
Possibly,

if you ignore pangs of guilt
built

from possibility of bacteria breath
death.

So what does one do?
Like Flu,

accept COVID as a once-yearly,
dearly

annoying friend who visits—wanted, or not?
The thought

provides a cold comfort paradigm.
In time,

an illness that's repeatable—infinitely
treatable

by over-the-counter,
any hour,

survives as pharmaceutical cash cow.
Now

that pandemic profitability is uttered,
nothing's shuttered.

Choice whether to wear mask is yours,
in stores

while you wait to purchase (and you will)
new COVI-Quil!

Speed Bumps in a Caring City

We're busy—absorbed
in our own problems
without answers. No time
to look up and discover
others suffer the same.

Privilege provides us
the luxury to complain.
A zero-sum use of time,
ranting and raving about
simple circular traffic patterns,
spewing vitriol over public art
installations added to enrich
the drudgery of the day-to-day
capitalist zombie commute.

Heads down, we try to maintain
liveable wages in step
with a rapacious inflation rate.
We earn the pay of our fathers,
yet provide less,
ask a stay-at-home-parent-by-choice
if you can find one.

Heads down, we dismiss
well-rounded education as superfluous,
believe learning is no more
than readin', writin', and 'rithmatic.
Passively, we permit and defend future-leader
sons and daughters to parade
in poverty clothes of other cultures
for school photo posterity,
the rich cultural tapestry ripping
apart at patchwork seams.

Heads down, we invite
refugees to begin again,
to diversify our city and economy,
yet offer them decrepit shelter
no better than camps fled
at supply-and-demand prices
greater than subsidies given,
cries for help in different tongues
fall on deaf resettlement ears,
leave them looking further west.

Wrapped in our choice
to ignore social responsibility,
we flout government and medical
requests to come together,
prevent unnecessary harm to all.
They infringe on the fashionable
decision to be coddled with misinformation.
The every-man-for-himself mantra is sexy
while you're on top, but
captains of corporations whistle
a different tune when tides turn
and they swim in panic
toward the social safety net.

Without fear of awkward
moments of misunderstanding,
we'd discover pain diminishes,
power multiplies in numbers
among the collective concerned.
It is possible to reach out,
burst secular bubbles to care
when neighbours are forced
to choose between a roof and food.

We can't just be in this
together when convenient.
It will feel weird
at first—to care.
Should we prefer
to remain comfortable,
remember what
our fathers said,
*Don't come crying
when you get hurt.*

The Promise of Home

I

Believe in the evidence,
it's out there, perhaps
in the very place you sit,
right now. The entire world
waiting for you to summon
the courage to say,

Hello.
How are you?
Where are you from?
This is what stands between
you and understanding,
between you and a friend.

In one room, you might experience—
China, Brazil, Iraq, Vietnam,
El Salvador, Romania, Cyprus,
England, Libya, Peru, and Turkey—
really experience, what it's like
to be a citizen abroad.

There's one catch.
To be more than tourist, or
voyeur, you must be ready
to listen, accept—
face fear of the unknown
across a table, over coffee.
This person will sound,
and look different than you.
But if you listen closely,
there will be points of access.

II

Frank IS a software engineer
from Shenzhen, China.
He's looking for work
while learning a difficult language.
Though his English is better
than a Frederictonian's Mandarin
or Cantonese, no one will give him
an opportunity to prove
skills and experience are not tied
to any one language.
Which prompts the question,
Might it be beneficial to be mute?

Sagida IS a lawyer. When she left Libya,
her lifetime of knowledge did not vanish
crossing borders. Yet here, in Fredericton,
what did disappear is her confident
courtroom stride, told too often
she does not qualify in her new home.

Lucy IS a musician, and
educator from Ningbo, China.
Currently a community volunteer.
An admirable pursuit—newcomer aiding,
integrating. But at a cost—
the submersion of cultivated identity.
Now given the simple description:
housewife. Unable to cut red tape,
pursue her *joie de vivre* in Fredericton.

Charles IS a journalist,
married to Lucy. He chose
Canada. Freed himself
from the anxious Chinese hamster
wheel of unattainable perfection.

As Charles sees it, he chose
the absurd, stress-free life
of cultural alien. Like an infant,
nothing to do but accept
help in every possible way.
An accomplished filmmaker,
he's happy in a country open
to the perceived frivolity of Art,
in a city friendly to fallibility
and reinvention.

III

Their stories ARE Fredericton's story.
What we view every day,
IS NOT a complete picture.
We choose what we want to see,
hear what we want to hear,
see STOP signs where there are none.
Personality, skill, and intellect transcend
bureaucratic language barriers.

We must exercise
atrophied empathy.
Ask our comfortable selves,
How it would feel
to be displaced,
lose everything, including
hard-earned identities?
We must help newcomers
fulfill this promise of home.

Eva Christensen
All the Redemption I Can Offer
is Beneath This Dirty Hood
2022

Watercolour on paper
14x18 inches

The Hardwood Comes to an Understanding
for Izzy Trethewey

I wish I were a Christmas Tree
then everyone would notice me.
Deep green bristles smartly shorn.
Dazzling decorations worn.

Wrapped around with strands of lights,
a welcome glow on winter nights.
Shiny star placed at my top—
a focal point when day is stopped.

Outside is where I shall remain,
December snow, and freezing rain.
My ornaments now blown away,
return again, on warm spring days.

Witnessed many Yuletides past
(don't ask, I'm terrible at math).
The cold puts me in hibernation
I never was one for vacation.

My shade, in summer, gives relief.
Among my branches robins tweet.
When Christmas rolls around each year,
I'm tempted into jaded sneer.

Holiday shrubs, again inside,
start poking at my leafless pride.
Yet I remain here, standing tall—
Winter, Spring, Summer, Fall.

Tag This!

Why do taggers tag—
is it just to brag?
Hey, look at me, I'm here!
I exist inside your sphere.

Are they angry, out of place—
detest others in their space?
Hate themselves, what they do,
want to drag the rest down, too.

Does a gang think it thrilling
hanging upside-down from buildings
scribbling symbols in the dark,
points based where they make a mark?

Is it Art, or vandalism—
should we send culprits to prison?
And fines will not be paid
by those who are afraid

to sign their real name,
play the pseudonym game.
Real artists sign their work,
don't make a city look like jerks.

Art installed in public space
for Dime Store Dali's to deface.
Racist rhetoric, vulgar verse
masking effort—the reverse.

Where's the root, what's the cause?
Should we put our lives on pause,
never express collective hope,
our hands tied with paint-pen rope?

If ownership's what taggers crave,
deface this poem, spray away!
Anonymous scribbles are weak.
Make some Art, don't be meek.

Ode to Your Postal Code (E3A 2B8) #1

Every day I walk up Fulton Avenue,
rain or shine.
Always around Nashwaaksis Middle School
with Texas
beside me checking pee-mail
from friends on cedar hedges we pass by.

Ode to Your Postal Code (E3A 2B8) #2

Even if I didn't live here
I would dream,
always, of walking out of a house like
this one
beside a neighbour like mine, on
a street in a town such as this.

Ode to Your Postal Code (E3B 1B8) #3

Elm City on the Wolastoq
we walk confidently
beside a life force freely
flowing
between
two halves of a whole lot of potential

Rebirth; Forgive Us Our Trespasses

For to-morrow can only fulfil
Dreams which to-day have birth[.]
—Bliss Carman, *A Creature Catechism*

Let's use hindsight to time travel back for
Fredericton's inception. City of tomorrow,
once Church of England claims skyline. Can
settler citizens acknowledge land can only
"belong" to all? Might fur trader and Loyalist DNA fulfill
promises of equity on both Wolastoq banks? Dreams
of parity among cultures on fertile territory which
we all share, call home—remain dreams today.
With 175 years of hindsight, these hopes have
to be reality. No more trespass. Collaborative birth.

Acknowledgements

"Essential Writing" first appeared in *Arc Poetry Magazine, 100.*

Thanks to my wife, Tina, and our children, Noah and Izzy, for sharing me with the city for three years.

Thanks to the Beaverbrook Art Gallery, and the Garrison Night Market, for the space and time to engage the community. Thanks to Angela Watson, Julia Stewart, Adda Mihailescu, and Zach Atkinson for their enthusiasm and support for this project. Thanks to Corenski Nowlan for being a faithful beta reader, and pal. Thanks to the Fredericton Public Library, Dog Eared Books, and Bookends, for keeping my books on their shelves...a dream come true.

Speaking of dreams fulfilled, a huge thank-you to Fredericton Mayor Kate Rogers, and members of Fredericton City Council, for giving me the opportunity to showcase and share my love of the written word with the community from 2021 to 2024 as the city's poet laureate. This is an honour and opportunity a little boy growing up in rural Nova Scotia in the Eighties and Nineties never thought possible. This boy sought adventure in the silence and excitement of stories...staking out secluded, sunny spots near abandoned railroad tracks to read. Now that boy will forever be a poet laureate from a Canadian capital city; a boy whose dream of writing words that matter came true.

Jordan Trethewey is the poet laureate of Fredericton, New Brunswick, Canada (2021-2024). He lives, writes, and works as a communications professional from his home in the suburb of Nashwaaksis, amidst by the comings and goings of his wife, son, and daughter. He is the author of four previous books of poetry (*Bathroom Stall Stanzas, Wishing on Satellites, Spirits for Sale, and Unexpected Mergers*), and a collection of short fiction (*Painfully Awkward*). *These Are the People in Your Neighbourhood* is the fulfillment of his legacy project for the City of Fredericton. He is currently editing his first novel among other writing projects.

To discover more of Jordan's work, please visit:
https://jordantretheweywriter.wordpress.com

Photo by Mag Hood Photography

Eva Christensen has been painting in watercolour for thirty years. She lives with her husband and their house full of dogs and cats near Fredericton, NB. These subjects and location are the frequent source of her painting inspiration.

Eva's work has also been featured in Created Here Magazine and on the cover of The Fiddlehead. Her work has been exhibited at the Charlotte Street Arts Centre in summer 2023 and featured in the On the Fence outdoor art installation curated by the Grassroots Gallery in Fredericton in 2021.

You can shop for prints of Eva Christensen's paintings at www.evachristensenart.etsy.com, and for a selection of original paintings exclusively at The Artisan District in beautiful downtown Fredericton, or www.artisandistrict.ca.

MORE ROADSIDE PRESS TITLES:

By Plane, Train or Coincidence
Michele McDannold

Prying
Jack Micheline, Charles Bukowski and Catfish McDaris

Wolf Whistles Behind the Dumpster
Dan Provost

Busking Blues: Recollections of a Chicago Street Musician and Squatter
Westley Heine

Unknowable Things
Kerry Trautman

How to Play House
Heather Dorn

Kiss the Heathens
Ryan Quinn Flanagan

St. James Infirmary
Steven Meloan

Street Corner Spirits
Westley Heine

A Room Above a Convenience Store
William Taylor Jr.

Resurrection Song
George Wallace

MORE ROADSIDE PRESS TITLES:

Nothing and Too Much to Talk About
Nancy Patrice Davenport

Bar Guide for the Seriously Deranged
Alan Catlin

Born on Good Friday
Nathan Graziano

Under Normal Conditions
Karl Koweski

Clown Gravy
Misti Rainwater-Lites

Walking Away
Michael D. Grover

All in a Pretty Little Row
Dan Provost